CELESTIAL INTERIM

BY

DOROTHY HOBSON

PARNASSUS PRESS
133 FURMAN STREET
BROOKLYN, N. Y.
MCMXXXIII

999 copies of "Celestial Interim,"
169 of which are numbered,
have been printed on a bulking book
paper from Caslon type set by hand
and the type has been distributed.

Designed and printed by LEW NEY
in his TYPE SHOP,
133 Furman St, Brooklyn, N. Y.

DEDICATION

O a young poet whose desire to create beauty always far outdistances his or her power of expression at any given stage of development, the encouragement of teachers, the friendliness of editors, the enthusiasm of readers, and the faith of relatives and intimates is priceless. When, as in the present instance, the same host of guardian angels add their financial help in publishing that young poet's first volume, conventional phrases of acknowledgment are utterly inadequate to convey the appreciation of the writer.

Above all, to my first friend, my mother, I am overwhelmingly grateful, not only for her lifelong unselfish devotion to me, but also for her remarkable expression of it in the exquisite little lyric which appeared in the New York American over a year ago:

SONG OF A POET'S MOTHER

Child of my heart, press on—
Sunder the shackles
With which I would bind thee;
Turn thy face to the dawn.

Child of my heart, soar high—
Long did I hold thee;
Now shall my cry be
Lift thy wings to the sky!

Child of my heart, go far—
Reach heights beyond me,
Out of my vision
(Nor shall my cry be
"Return," for I love thee);
Follow the light of a star!

MATHILDA C. HOBSON

I can only say to her, and to all the rest of you whose names follow: If loyalty to an ideal can effect its realization, my work shall one day fulfil your confidence in me. In the meantime, search this book (which is only a beginning), not for what it is in the flesh, but what it strove to be in the spirit. For now it is not my book, but YOURS:

Adeline C. Bartlett, Mignon Barton, Conrad J. Benneck, Mrs. Fred Bowen, Mr & Mrs. Gilbert Boyd, Bertha Briggs, Marie Donaldson Brown, Laura M. Carleton, Dr. Charles W Chandler, Dora Christmann, Samuel Collins, Viola E Comstock, Anne L. Corbitt, Catherine Cossum, Irma Csinos, Hazel Dean, Ruth Minar Dowd, Anna Stewart Ellis, Estella Rose Fisher, Elliot W Fiske, Alfred Fitzgerald, Mrs A W Flannigan, Alta Fogelgren, Keith Fowler, George Garrott, Fred Gudnitz, Frederic P Gutekunst, Mildred Hackney, Vera Hale, Hayner Library, Alton, Ill., (Jane Bassett), Edgar F. Higgins, Jr, Dr A. Augustus Hobson, Ruth Hobson, Virginia Hobson, Prof Inez L Hollingsworth, LeAnna Howlett, Stanley Johnson, Elsie D Lane, Erma C Lane, William Largent, Marion Light, Dr Thomas Ollive Mabbott, Harriet McClintock, George V A. McCloskey, Francis L McCrudden, Mrs. Cora Megowen, Dr. H. E Middleton, John E Moll, S. L Moore, Angela Murphy, Gertrude Murrell, Benjamin Musser, Helen Ober, James O'Donnell, Virginia Olive, Carrie Parker, Richard L Phillips, Carnegie W Pullen, Mrs. James Reardon, Florence Miller Reid, Robley Book Shop, Philip F Rohrbach, Stanley H. Saunders, South Junior High School Library, Waltham, Mass, Robert Stebbins, Prof George N Stevenson, Lois A. Stevenson, Mrs. Henry Stewart, Frank J Stobbs, Mary Sullivan, Sally Tanenbaum, Prof Emma K. Temple, Charles Hanson Towne, Peter Traverso, Elsie E Turner, Marjorie Volkers, Anca Vrbovska, George L Ward, Rev John A. Wade, Sigmund Weiss, Lillian F Weller, Ethel White, Prof Claire V Whiting, Ruth Widén, Luther Emanuel Widén, Jean T Wilde, Dr Blanche Colton Williams, Gertrude D. Winder, & Mary L Wyckoff.

THE POEMS

Part 4

Part 5

I

"THE ONE REMAINS. . ."

CELESTIAL INTERIM

I

O sweet, how wildly I have searched for you,
Ever since first I felt my sharp-prowed bark
Of death scrape lightly on the glittering blue
Crescent of heaven's edge, and scanned the arc
Of shore for sight of you, where all was stark,
Shining and empty: yet I did not fear;
I thought: "Soon I shall find him, as a lark
Finds the great sky, and sooner will he hear
My heart's glad carol mounting to him blithe and clear."

II

High on a crystal cliff God smiled at me
And waved His hand, whose motion spun quick rays
Of rose and copper fire, as fleetingly
As hills are warm with dawn's soft vivid haze

Or evening mist may hold the sunset-blaze;
While fond celestial sparks like gems were shed
Over me as I passed into the maze
Of tall blue sand-dunes, and I shook my head:
"He will not know me with these jewels on," I said. . .

III

I left the shore and scaled the breathless slope
To aery terraces where I discerned
Towers of sapphire; tremulous with hope,
I sought the bright-robed crowds with eyes that yearned
Fiercely upon each face and, failing, turned
Even from smiles of those long-lost and dear;
On, on I sped, till all my being burned
With newborn anguish, and a subtle fear
Whispered: "This is not Heaven if he is not here. . ."

IV

In elfin byways and Elysian nooks
And gardens gay with flower-fantasies
I searched; in calm rooms, rich with precious books
Penned by the masters of the centuries,
And halls wherein immortal pageantries
Are staged; then, in the stately city square
Where orchestras were luring symphonies
From weird and wondrous strings, I paused to stare
At every player's face—but all were strangers there.

V

Trembling, I ran beyond the city's rim
Out into meadows starred with asphodel;
Through sylvan hollows, ferny, cool and dim,
Past shadowed pools where waterlilies dwell;

Down sheer ravines where swift blue cascades fell;
Wherever were still caverns to explore
In river-gorge or chasm's rocky well,
I sought you, but stern silence loomed before
The eyes of hope like an impenetrable door.

VI

On, on I journeyed, over fertile plains,
Through mammoth forests, limitless and dense,
Across vast mountain ranges, linked in chains
Of ice-spired summits, blazing like immense
Streamers of frozen comets in the intense
Brilliance of myriad suns; upon one crest
I stopped, and in the lone magnificence
Of light I leaned against a crag to rest
And, sobbing, clung to it as if it were your breast.

VII

"Dear love," I whispered, "never shall my feet
Falter, till every dell of Paradise
Be worn to desert with their passing, sweet;
You are my Heaven, and my heart defies
The mandate of a cosmos that denies
Breath to the living, immortality
To the immortal: Eden's boundless skies
Are not so wide but that love's sorcery
Shall find you where you are and give you back to me—

VIII

"And I shall find you, darling, though my hands
Must tear apart each rock, uproot each tree,
Batter the very hills, until there stands
No wall, no corner of infinity

Untracked, unscarred or unassailed by me;
Though I must cry to God upon His height
That Hell with hope of seeing you would be
Sweeter than this Elysium's bleak delight,
Praying that I be hurled with you into the night. . ."

IX

Lightning! and far beyond my storm of tears
I heard a sudden angry thunder groan;
Nearer it came and fiercer, till the spheres
Shook in their orbits, cliffs began to moan,
Oceans congealed, and giant trees fell prone,
Fearing that Voice, whose whisper might create
A universe, whose cataclysmic Tone
Descended on me with the awful weight
Of Wrath Omnipotent become articulate:

X

"What is that note of wild discordant pain
Amid my harmonies? What rebel rune
Disrupts the music of my fair Domain
Where not a block of building stone is hewn
Save from a willing rock, nor petal strewn
Within my path, save from a loving flower?
Who dares to throw a Heaven out of tune,
And for what mighty Cause, and by whose power
Hopes he to shield himself from Me this fateful hour?"

XI

The Godhead paused; Eternity stood still,
Expectant—but I could not break the spell
That bound me speechless yet against my will;
And then—oh, then I heard across the well

Of black a strong voice, silver as a bell,
Mellow with beauty cherished long ago
Upon the Earth, now lifting me from Hell
To the one Heaven I shall ever know:
"Why are You angry, Father? Who displeased You so?"

XII

I raised my eyes, bewildered and amazed
To see God's face, bright, tranquil, in the sky;
The clouds were gone, the empyrean blazed
With rainbow flashings; on a hill nearby
You stood, the dearest form that tender eye
Of mortal or of angel ever scanned,
Listening gravely while God asked you why
You were neglecting missions you had planned—
Or had the distance back from earth so soon been spanned?

XIII

In trance of ecstasy, I felt your words
Of brave reply but dimly, loving more
The music of your speaking, sweet as birds
At morning, soft as oak-leaves' murmured lore,
Strong as the beat of ocean on its shore:
"Father, I did set out; but when I was halfway
Over the silver gulf, I heard Your roar
Of thunder far, far off across the bay;
I feared that You might need me... Will You let me stay?"

XIV

God nodded gently; then His shining glance
Fell suddenly on me where still I dreamed
In happy silence—sharply as a lance
At first; but all at once there gleamed
Within His eyes twin dawns of Love, that streamed

Over the crags, rose-luminous and mild;
And when you ran to meet me,sweet, it seemed
As if I heard Him whisper, as He smiled
At me: "Ah, well — you always were impatient, Child. . ."

2

"The many change and pass. . ."

FOR A LITTLE WHILE

Belovèd, do not say the warm words yet,
Nor reach your hand to touch me; only let
Unspoken beauty flash from heart to heart
Uncertainly, as frail young birdlings start
On shining untried wings; oh, fling no net
Of mad sweet words to capture me, but let
There close about me for a little while
Only the slow enchantment of your smile. . .

New York American

BLUE SOIL

If I had cast this seed in common earth,
Then, though dark soil triumphantly gave
birth
To flowers colorful and frail and rare,
Still would I crush them in my two hands, tear
The fragile rootlets from the warm black
ground,
Destroy them utterly, because you frowned
Upon them, scorned a beauty born so low—
This would I do, if I had sown it so.

But since the seed I held was like a star,
I went away; and oh, I wandered far,
Running knee-deep in planets, till I found
A bare sky-field. Into the soft blue ground
I thrust my seed, and there a tall star-tree
Stands showering silver blossoms lavishly
On purple loam. . . My dear, how can I do
This thing: wrench long white roots from
soil of blue,
Tear down a tree that scatters stars for you?

WHOSE VOICE IS BEAUTY

God, I am tired of standing on the shore
And looking toward one ship that passes by
Too far away to hear a yearning cry
Whose sound is lost within the breakers' roar;
And I am tired of waiting at a door
That will not open to me in my need
Though I have beat and beat with hands that bleed,
Hurt hands that shall be raised to knock no more.

Oh, human hearts are cruel—let me rest
A little while upon the tender breast
Of Love that quivers through the flowered sod,
That throbs in sunlight and the white still shine
Of stars—upon Your breast, O Love divine
Whose voice is Beauty and whose name is God.

WINTER SUNSET
A Cinquain Sequence

Outlined
Against a wall
Of gold, black cloud-horses
Gallop down the vermilion road
To death.

How strange
The outer shell
Of me should thus live on
As if it did not know my heart
Were dead.

The tree,
Once stirred to songs
Of joy by summer winds,
Now, bare of leaves, can only moan
In pain.

My heart,
Why did you break
In winter? Were it June,
The warm beauty of summer might
Heal you.

LOST ILLUSION

Bring me the pilgrim staff, the dusty shoes
  I laid away: I must resume the Quest
(Oh, I was sure I would not need to use
  Them any more—I thought that I might
      rest);

Be brave, heart: we are not the first to know
  The Holy Grail, then have it disappear;
(But oh, the grief to see a vision go
  That was so heavenly-fair, so wondrous
      near. . . .)

New York American

LET IT BE REMEMBERED

Oh, let it be remembered; let its cost
Be blotted out—the anguish and the sting
Of unshed tears—but not the lovely thing
Itself; nor let the happy dream be lost
Because the wakening was chill as frost:
Let me keep this, as I have loved to sing
Of dawn-fires long since faded, burying
Remembrance of dark days all tempest-
tossed.

There is a Beauty like the sun, so bright
One cannot gaze for long, but one may cling
Forever to the memory of a far
White vision, as upon a cloudy night
Still woodland waters dream, remembering
How they once held the image of a star.

SONG AFTER LOVING

I was a taper white;
You were the flame that gave
The candle all its light.

I was a singing tree;
You were the wind that stirred
Its leaves to melody. . .

Now in the silence and the dark of night
A slim white taper mourns for lost delight,
For vanished radiance of leaping fire
That was at once fulfilment and desire;
A still tree droops, remembering the long
Swift ecstasy that thrilled it once with song. . .

But dark shall pass and silence break: your name
Shall be forgotten; to the drooping tree
Shall wander other wind, and there shall be
Light for the taper from another flame.

The Step Ladder

MILK-CART

Cool breath of dawn-winds
Stir night's heat;
A milk-cart clotters
Down the street;
The sound awakens
Ancient pain,
An old wound reddens
To a stain:

The night I waited, a twelve-months bride,
For you, whose very love had lied;
Till dawn, kept vigil, terrified,
For you, our baby at my side.

My son is sturdy,
Straight and tall,
Nor knows you never
Came at all

Home to his mother
  Waiting there;
He does not know you,
  Does not care.

The love I gave you long is dead;
And now beside me in my bed
Sleeps a new lover, brave and true,
Fit to be father more than you;

Of that old heartbreak
  There remain
Only these fleshless
  Bones of pain,
That stir at a milk-cart's
  Clottering sound
And go on sleeping
  Under the ground.

CHANGE IS BEAUTY

If, blind with ardor, I have ever yearned
To stay the fleeting ecstasy, to hold
The color of a rose, a sunset's gold,
I shall no more. For I have lately learned
A strange new truth; I read it as it burned
White in the strong lined faces of the old;
I heard the planets sing it as they rolled,
The shifting seasons chant it while they turned.

And I shall worship changelessness no more,
Since I have found a meaning in the sight
Of darkness giving eager birth to light,
The ebb and flow of tides upon the shore,
For life shall flame forever with this strange
Bright thought: that change is beauty, beauty change.

Contempo

3

" . . . A DOME OF MANY-
COLORED GLASS. . . "

TO MY LITTLE BOY, AWAY

If I could have you back, I would not say
"I am too busy,"—oh, how we would play
Together, games so quaint, so wondrous new
That you would laugh out loud, and having you
So near, so gay, I should be merry, too. . .

I would not scold you when you touched my dress
With dirty fingers in a clumsy warm caress;
How I would hold your little weary head
Against my heart; and when you were in bed
How I would tell you stories, fairy-schemes
And giant-lore, till you were lost in dreams. . .

EVEN IN THIS PLACE

(Written at Roxana, Illinois, 1929)

I never dreamed I should find Beauty here,
Bleak village born of oil refineries;
When first I saw you with your stunted trees,
Your small box-houses, and your fields all sere
And brown, there came to me a stifling fear
Lest I should shrivel and go barren, too,
Waiting for Beauty, listening with you
In vain to hear her voice speak sweet and clear.

But now I know that even in this place
May Loveliness step softly, singing low,
Since I have seen black chimneys, tall and stark,
Spread smoky veils across the dawn's flushed face—
Since I have seen white oil-tanks, in the glow
Of moon, shine silverly against the dark.

Contemporary Verse

NETS OF SINGING WORDS

I could spread nets of singing words for you—
But you would smile and gracefully slip through
The closely-woven meshes; I could say
That you are light that glimmers far away
Mistily blue on winter hills, in space
Where sun and snow cling in a white embrace,
Each breathless, calling on the other's name;
Or I could say you are a blade of flame
Hid in a sheath of dreams, or you are slow
Silver of silent-passing stars that go
Looking for beauty in the dim blue night...
These words would almost hold you, but not quite:
These would be closely knit and bright and true,
But there would always be still more of you—
More loveliness—and more—that would slip through...

OVER THE HILLS

OVER the hills
Came walking two:
One was the Spring
And one was you,
But both so fair
I never knew
(Though my love for both
Was sweet and true
And made me sing)
Which one was you
And which was Spring.

New York American

TO JOYCE KILMER

This, then, is glorious War: the brutal scythe
That mowed the lilies down with grass and weed,
That swept your flower-spirit on to feed
Insatiable mouths of guns, to writhe
Between the jaws of Hell; that broke your lithe
Young body, and denied a world in need
Of Beauty when it stilled your soul's clear reed
Within the middle of its measure blithe.

Ten million strong sweet lives—that were a price
Alone too great, enough of penance sore
To have atoned for all this blind world's sin
And greed, without this added sacrifice,
This cruel blotting out of all your store
Of carolled loveliness that might have been.

JAPM: The Poetry Weekly

LEST YOUR OWN HEART BREAK

Mother who bore her, look not deep
Into her eyes lest you should weep,
Perceiving she has come to know
What you discovered long ago:

Life's cup is sweet
And one may laugh
Who lightly sips
Or drinks but half;
The cup is sweet,
But dregs are gall,
As one may learn
Who drains it all.

If she should pass from out your door,
Knowing she shall return no more,
Mother who bore her, let her go,
And take no notice of her woe.

Make no farewell, nor any moan,
When she fares forth, frail and alone,

With one dim candle-flame to light
The wintry darkness of her night,
(The taper of a memory
Of lips that loved her recklessly
Once, once when Spring and love were true
And nights were warm and starry-blue. . .)

Mother who bore her, you must let
Her go. This is her wish: forget
You had a daughter, do not mourn
Her babe that shall be homeless born.

(Life's cup is sweet
And one may laugh
Who lightly sips
Or drinks but half;
The cup was sweet,
But dregs are gall,
As one has learned
Who drained it all)

Mother who bore her, turn away
Your searching eyes, nor bid her stay;
Her heart has died, but you must take
No notice, lest your own heart break.

NEW MOON

There shall never be sorrow of mine so deep
That the pain of it may not be sung to sleep
By a new moon caught in a warm sunset
Like a sliver of pearl in a flaming net. . .

ON BEGINNING TO LEARN GERMAN

As children, born on alien soil, might go
When orphaned, back to their ancestral home
To live; as, on the first day, they might roam
Beneath the timeless elm trees, hearing low
Voices of ancient kinsmen in the flow
Of wind through singing leaves; as they might thrill
Glimpsing a fern-sweet dell, a graceful hill,
Enchantments they may soon explore and know:

So I am filled with echoings today,
Waked by the mellow music of this tongue
My mother's forbears spoke, in which were sung
Their prayers, their dreams, their loves; so I survey
Glories of Goethe and of Heine hung
Like magic heights beyond a sun-lit way.

BALLAD

Faith, Hope, and Love, the gentle three,
Before God's throne,
Pleading for frail humanity,
Made tender moan:

"Man suffers, for the elements
Are too unkind;
Add to his dower, for defense
A keen-edged mind."

God bowed His shining head and wept;
When ceased the storm,
"Reason!" He called, and forth there stepped
A tall armed form.

His sword was long and sharp and new,
His stride was fast:
To earth he sped and mightier grew
As ages passed.

There came a time when all was won:
Nature was chained;
But, though the destined task was done,
Reason remained.

One day Man saw the armored slave
Digging a pit;
Shallow it was, and like a grave;
Man stared at it.

A second hole the warrior made,
And then one more;
Wielding his sword-edge like a spade,
He laughed and swore.

He laughed and swore with joy to hear
Man's trembling cry:
"If these be graves that you dig here,
Then tell me why;

"Then tell me all the meaning of
Your wild weird glee. . ."
"These are for Faith and Hope and Love
Who summoned me,

"While this last grave," the conqueror said,
As he began
To dig the fourth dark earthy bed,
"Is yours, O Man."

OCTOBER MORNING IN NEW YORK

Long shafts of autumn sunlight edge their way
Shyly between tall buildings. Taxis spin
Designs of gold, maroon, and silver-gray
In crowded streets; amid the dust and din
The people hurry, tense and worn and white,
Shading tired eyes from blaze of morning light.

(At home, today, the maples will be flame
Leaping to skies of vivid blue; the same
Sun will be spilling lakes of gold between
Long quiet shadows on still lawns of green. . . .)

TO A LOVELY STRANGER

Why came you here, fair goddess of the hills?
If I had found you in a secret glade
Serenely gathering frail white lilies made
Of moonbeams, or tall-poised between two rills
Upon whose singing waters Autumn spills
Gold coins of sunlight from an amber spade—
I would have smiled, nor felt this keen afraid
Wonder that through my startled being thrills:

In this drab wilderness of walls you are
Only a mad mirage, a wild sweet dream
That soon will vanish; but I would have known
That you were real, had I beheld you far
Among the hills beside a singing stream,
Counting out coins of sunlight on a stone.

TO MY MOTHER

There is no heart so gallant or so gay
So bravely plumed and armored for the fray,
But that it knows defeat, the wound, the pain,
The shame of loss, the breastplate's red-
dening stain.

This is the strange, the secret fate of all:
There is no man so bold, so proud, so tall
But in fierce sorrow or the fevered strain
Of illness shall become a child again;
This is the common lot, that in the stark
Loneliness of frustration, through the dark
The soul cries out to that which it may name
Mother or God—the yearning is the same:

The dim desire to be warmly drawn
Close to the heart of Love which is the dawn
And night of being—love which once it knew

Most nearly (could the soul remember) through
Those tender days within the quiet womb. . .

So shall each heart cry out, and so shall mine
Ever in dark torn moments, nor define
If it be calling God or you, my dear;
Thus shall my soul yearn, dreaming of the year
When nearest to the love of God I grew
Because I lay beneath the heart of you.

ON PASSING THE CHRYSLER BUILDING

Unwise it is to come too near
Great men or stately monuments, to peer
Up the long sheer expanse of face:
One cannot see the spire from the base.

CHRISTMAS

This is the time of year when hearts delve
deep
Into a precious store of loves asleep
And friendships wrapped in silence; when
with these
Delicate-bright and sparkling memories,
We deck life's sturdy boughs of evergreen;
This is the time of year when faces seen
In happy hours, smiling come again
To press against the spirit's window-pane,
Adding the radiance of their tender mirth
To candles lit there for the Christ-child's
birth.

4

"... THE WHITE RADIANCE
OF ETERNITY..."

ADVENT

I thought that it would come with sudden blare
Of many trumpets, and the bursting flare
Of vivid colors, gold and flame and blue,
All blended in a strange and wondrous hue
Of blinding glory; but it has been born
As quietly and simply as the morn
Who enters, singing softly as she goes,
Clad in a misty gown of palest rose,
A-stepping lightly on the eastern hills
And leans to kiss the rivers and the rills
From sleep—so tranquilly it came to me,
With all the life-bequeathing mystery
Of common daylight, that my senses grow
All hushed in reverent wondering to know
There should be born in me a joy so bright,
As simply as a white dawn follows night.

TALL TREES

There are tall trees that seem to tower high
Toward the stars with upward-straining ear
Attuned to whisperings from a purer sphere;
But there are winds that rush a-shouting by
And shake the trees that dare to touch the sky,
With fury spared to those less tall and sheer
Who, ignorant of storms, may wondering hear
Far, far above their heads a singing cry.

Let me grow tall toward stars that blend their slight
Voices for me in chorus frail and high
And play upon the purple harp of night
With fingers slow and thin and silver-white—
Oh, let me grow, though winds come running by
And find me tall and lone against the sky.

New York American

I DO NOT BELIEVE THEM

They tell me, God, that some day You will
raise
Your mighty fist and smash the world You
made;
They tell me this . . . but I am not afraid;
For I have come to know Your heart, Your
ways,
Oh, better far than they: long nights and days
Have I spent looking up into Your eyes,
Lost in the blue and wistful deeps of wise
And lovely dreams that glimmer in Your gaze.

Your eyes were wistful when You made the
world,
Your heart was wild with hope. . . What
though the gleam
Seem far as then? You will not break Your
dream;
—Or if with thoughtless move You ever hurled
It down to dust, I know how You would
stand
And gather the broken bits into Your hand. . .

TO KEATS

Why did you let them quench you, heart of fire?—
For you were stronger than your enemies
Of Poverty and Grief and grim Disease,
If you had only known. O spirit-lyre,
You were, of all who ever did aspire
To search for Beauty's grail, the only knight
Deemed pure enough to glimpse the sacred light;
You gained, had you but known, your heart's desire:

Now are dissolved the dusty names of those
Who crushed you, as the mist beneath the sun,
The while a world adoring hails you one
Supremely honored, one whom Beauty chose,
From centuries of kings and lordly peers,
To sound her silver trumpet down the years.

DO NOT WONDER

To Benjamin Musser

You gave me wingèd sandals for my feet
That bore me running up a wide blue stair
To shining fields of far enchantment where
Slim Beauty wanders in her still retreat,
Plucking the sunset-flowers and the sweet
Blossoms of dawn, and twines them in her hair,
And links the stars in bracelets for her fair
White arms—the shoes you gave were wondrous fleet.

You gave me wingèd footsteps for that stair;
Then do not wonder greatly that I bring
Back to you tribute from that far blue land:
A fragile flower caught from Beauty's hair
(Oh, do not crush it) and a jewelled ring
Borrowed for you from an immortal hand.

I SAW A MOUNTAIN HEIGHT—

Once, in a dream, I saw a mountain height
So lofty that its crest was hid from sight
In clouds no mortal eye could penetrate;
I saw, below, a city through whose gate
A mighty throng pressed forth to scale the bleak
And stony slopes toward the unseen peak.
The striving ranks were crowded, near the base;
But higher, where the mountain's craggy face
Grew steeper, and a sweeping wintry gale
Blew fiercely, one by one I saw them quail...

I watched the few who dared yet to ascend:
From time to time I saw one turn and bend
His gaze down through blue space upon a scene
Wide as eternity, beheld him lean
To shout at laggards on the level ground

Who never heard. Still climbed these few: each wound
His way among sharp crags, till finally
They lost each other, and were hid from me,
As they approached the sheer and awful place
Where cloud met rock. There did not one retrace
His steps; each struggled on alone, uncheered. . .
But once I heard one call out in a weird
Cry of doomed loneliness, and my heart broke,
Hearing no answer. . . Weeping, I awoke. . .

LADFN TREE

Beneath the Tree of night one might go mad
With hunger for the star-fruit glittering
Among the purple leaves; one's heart might break
With hopeless waiting for those boughs to fling
Their lustrous burden down—oh, do not stare
So wildly, yearning for a silver pear—
Oh, do not linger vainly dreaming there:

Go on your way before it is too late,
Leave the dark shadow of the laden Tree—
You might forget that star-fruit is not ripe
Till autumn-harvest of Eternity,
When only lips immortal may aspire
To taste—you might go mad with weird desire
For pears of unattainable white fire.

PALACE OF LIGHT

To H. D.

O Lovely, all last night I dreamed of you;
And as you wandered glamorously through
My happy vision, suddenly fulfilled
Were all the sweet mad yearnings which have
thrilled
My spirit since the wild unearthly light
Of Beauty Unattainable poured bright
Upon me from the radiance of your fair,
Your perfect face, the halo of your hair:

Each fantasy of too-sublime desire
That seared my helpless mortal heart with fire
Ethereal, took form; in Fairyland,
Upon a dune of iridescent sand
Stroked by the jewelled fingers of a lake
That murmured of her love, God let me make
A cloud-tall Palace out of light for you:
Rooms of white moon-mist, ceilinged with
the blue

Of skies at dusk whose color, like a rose,
From palest sapphire at horizon flows
Deepening to purple petals laid apart
To show star-stamens at the blue-black heart;

Wide chambers panelled with the golden haze
That mellow late October warmly lays
Over her lustrous fruits, her yellow sheaves;
Walls hung with tapestries the sunset weaves
On opalescent looms; long corridors
Carpeted with the sunny-dappled floors
Of woods in summer; chapels calm, austere,
Roofed with the astral brilliance, stinging clear
Of cloudless heavens on a winter night;
And over one great hall of breathless height
The rare aurora borealis blew
Bubbles of mauve, soft green, or crimson hue.

There, to that place made precious to deserve
Your smile, you came, across the rainbow curve

Which spanned a moat smooth-silver with
the veils
That luminous Diana slowly trails
Over still ocean-waters; there you came
Unto my altar like a holy flame;
And for an hour by grace of Heaven was mine
All loveliness, both earthly and divine,
That, kneeling, I might lay it at your feet
In the hushed glory of that pure retreat.

How the dull shock of morning cracked the
bell
Of beauty absolute, I shall not tell,
Nor how in that chill dawn I could but weep
And plead, "If this be waking, let me sleep
Forever, or if that perfection be
The true, the ultimate one reality,
Let me no more be exiled in this maze
Of phantom flesh, of spectral hours and
days—"

Never with that sad sequel shall my soul
Darken your spirit's vivid aureole;
But I shall sing, O Loveliest, to you
Only of how a holy vision grew
From seeds of fancy, so that you may smile,
Remembering how I built, upon a pile
Of lake-lapped sand, ephemeral towers of light
Where you were worshipped all one dreaming night.

EVENING WALK

So many roads are calling me tonight—
Ways that are easy—winding highways white
Whose smoothness beckons to my tired
feet. . .
White roads, I cannot go. I hear a sweet
And silver call upon the wind, the cry
Of smoke that follows down the evening sky
A trail that I must follow too, or die;

The brown way, then, the rutted road for me
That points toward unknown goals the
smoke-wraiths see,
The hidden Gleam beyond the purple-gray
Of dusk; for me, the yearning silent way
The long smoke travels, while the deep rose-
glow
Of sunset melts to mauve and star-points
show;
For me, the dreaming way the smoke-lines
go:

This is the trail that I would follow on
Through twilight into dark, through night
to dawn,
Although the path be rough, although my feet
Be weary; this the trail whose silver-sweet
Wild call my heart must answer all my days;
And when you cannot find me in white ways,
Look far on roads that point where long
smoke strays.

DISCORD

Tonight there is a note that jars
The stately music of the stars;

It is my heart all out of tune,
My wild heart crying for a boon
That is not written there for me
Upon the score of destiny. . .

O sobbing heart, draw tight your string
So that hereafter, when you sing,
You mar the cosmic symphony
With no wild lonely melody. . .

5

To A. F.

"... MUSIC, WORDS, ARE WEAK
THE GLORY THEY TRANSFUSE WITH
FITTING TRUTH TO SPEAK."

SILENCE WOULD BE UNBEARABLE

Little I thought a human voice could be
Soft as the long low murmuring of rain;
Little I dreamed a voice could wake in me
Wild echoes of that ancient wondering pain
Stirred by the measured music of the sea:

Not learning this, have I borne patiently
These years of silence, but henceforth I fear
Silence would be unbearable to me
Now that I know a voice may be as dear
As long low rain-song or the singing sea.

New York American

FIRESIDE

Many a million years may bear me far
From you, this fire, this copper bowl's warm sheen;
A million long blue miles may reach between;
But, in the crystal coolness of some star,
I shall be still remembering; fate may bar
Your way from mine forever up the slope
Of immortality, yet one frail hope
Shall burn upon my bosom like a scar.

Since Beauty made this moment for us now,
Eternity itself cannot erase
The memory of your kiss upon my brow:
Aeons from now, in some still starry place
I shall be loving you, and dreaming how
Radiantly this firelight touched your face.

New York American

LEST IN THE VALE'S DELIGHT

Now God must try my soul in lesser ways
Lest in the unaccustomed splendid blaze
Of this love-miracle mine eyes go blind
To subtler cosmic rays they once divined;
Lest in the amber glory of your eyes
I lose the blue perspective of cold skies.

More certainly than sorrow, joy lays bare
The soul to danger; therefore let me fare
Roughly in other ways, since now for me
Burns in your face the ultimate ecstasy;
Lest in the vale's delight I yearn to seek
No more the stark blue beauty of the peak.

PEACE

Serenity of hills, proud mystery
Of ancient trees—these have been dear to me,
And often with a lover's wild regret
Amid the city's noise and alien fret
Of strange confusions, have I wept for these:
The calm of hills, the quiet of old trees.

But now I shall not need them any more;
Let dark walls tower, let the city roar—
I shall not weep, for I have found my peace:
You are my mountains and my quiet trees.

You are the music of a hidden stream
Singing beneath the intermittent gleam
Of sun through drooping leaves; you are the still
Holiness of a dim sweet forest dell
Where, in the hush, frail hands unbar for me
A door that opens to Eternity;

You are the deep blue dark of starry nights,
The tall white stillness of far mountain
heights. . .
Though I have loved calm hills and quiet trees,
I have found peace: I have no need of these.

TO ONE WHO IS NEAREST OF ALL

Tonight it seems
The distant gleams
Of the farthest star
Are not so far
As you from me,
And eternity
Is not so long
As years my song
Would roam the blue
Till heard by you.

ENCHANTED WOOD

Only as two might wander for an hour
Within a magic wood, may you and I
Know earth's warm ways of loving, fortify
Cool tangencies of spirit with the power
And pain of throbbing pulses, whose sweet dower
This world, of all the worlds, uniquely brings
To lovers on immortal journeyings
That pause, enchanted, in her leafy bower.

Come, take my hand, love; quickly let us trace
The shape of each blue shadow, note the curve
Of brooks, breathe deep of fragrance, let each nerve
Tense with the earth-born beauty of this place—
—Hush—even now, beyond the mist-cool hills
For us, far-echoing, a silver trumpet thrills. . .

LOVE SONG

Bury the secret deep, deep,
Under the hearth, let thick vines creep
Over the roof; let strangers find
A locked door and a close-drawn blind:
Let them depart with puzzled face,
Not knowing this a magic place,
Nor that, when they have gone, the ground
Will shake with lilting silver sound
Of elfin laughter; cottage walls
Will change again to palace halls;
The thatchèd roof will disappear;
Above, enchanted towers will rear
Nine shimmering spires into the blue—
An ancient fairy-tale come true.

This unbelieving world, immune
To loveliness, and all in tune
With doubt, must never stare upon
This marvel; no incredulous one

May glimpse this miracle that came
To set our lives' dead wood aflame;
Bury the secret, hide its gleam—
Strangers will not believe the dream;
Wonder of shining lofty spire,
Vanish; enchanted clean hearth-fire,
Be smoke, when alien feet draw near:
Let all who, curious, enter here
Find in this magic place no more
Than a drawn blind and a bolted door.

PLANET

So long as there are suns, and worlds that run
A dreaming course of life about each sun,
So long shall I within my orbit-space
Look with desire upon your far bright face.

ONE PLACE

One place there is, one far immortal clime
 Where you are mine forever; though the tide
 Of music that once bore you to my side
Should swell again; though, drowning love's low chime
Of bells beneath the violins' sublime
 Yearning refrain, the waters should divide
 Us each from each, yet ever shall abide
We two in lands of Beauty for all time.

In that far place is gathered everything
 Precious that I have broken carelessly
Or lost, all loveliness to which I cling—
And there (though sad the strain great waves may sing)
 Proudly amid that gracious company
 Always with eyes alight you walk with me.

TURN NOT FROM THESE

You who are more to me than breath, turn not
From these my kisses, sorrowing that I prize
The pulses' warmth too highly nor despise
The body's earthy symbols. Probe this thought:
That never for their own sake have I sought
The evanescent blisses of the flesh
But for delight that in our passion's mesh
The spirit's wild bright birds are often caught.

Then—as lost gulls above the ocean's foam
Love winds that shoreward bear their tired wings;
As travelers bless the fragrance of a flower
That stirs a yearning in their hearts for home—
Cherish the body's swift desire that brings
Our wandering souls together for an hour.

WILDERNESS

My soul is lost upon a lonely plain
Of indescribable confusions, stirred
By your blunt utterance of a crucial word:
All Hell is spread, a wilderness of pain
Where, shivering naked in the sleety rain
Blown by wild icy winds, with vision blurred
By snow and tears, I wander, having heard
Truth that lies dark within me like a stain.

Then do not stand there grieving, sweet, for me
I have no other teacher than this pain;
These are my textbooks: Hell set free,
The gale, the blizzard, and the freezing rain:
I shall be wiser than I used to be
When I come out into the sun again.

WITH YOU

I need not fear the years will be
Ever too safe, too dull for me
Of the wild heart, the untamed soul:
Our love will keep its fairest goal
Unreached forever, though we cease
To wander, though we capture peace
As hushed as sleep; my life with you
Will always bear the glamorous hue
Of perilously lovely flight
Through skies of shifting cloud and light.

CHANGE IS NOT ALL OF BEAUTY

Once, in the dawn of wisdom's youth, I wrote
"Beauty is change;" by sight of truth struck blind
I saw its one side only. Now I find
Change is not all of beauty: one may note
With wonder shifting shapes of cloud that float
Upon the breast of sunlight—till the wind
Rend them, unveiling suddenly, behind,
The peaks of mountains, dreaming, poised, remote.

Let youth, then, learn the loveliness of change,
In transient moods of earth, in deaths that are
The opening of new doors; but age will see
The miracle that carved the mountain range:
Eternal beauty binding star to star,
Mother to little child, and you to me.

Harper's Magazine

CPSIA information can be obtained
at www.ICGtesting.com
Printed in the USA
BVOW04s2001061216
469962BV00017B/181/P